WALTZING THE WILARRA

WRITTEN & COMPOSED BY DAVID MILROY

Currency Press
Sydney

YIRRA
YAAKIN
THEATRE COMPANY

CURRENCY PLAYS

First published in 2011
by Currency Press Pty Ltd,
PO Box 2287, Strawberry Hills, NSW, 2012, Australia
enquiries@currency.com.au
www.currency.com.au
in association with
Yirra Yaakin Theatre Company, Perth.
Copyright © David Milroy, 2011.

Reprinted in 2017, 2018

NATIONAL LIBRARY OF AUSTRALIA CIP DATA

Author: Milroy, David.
Title: Waltzing the Wilarra / David Milroy.
ISBN: 9780868199092 (pbk.)
Dewey Number: A822.4

Typeset by Dean Nottle for Currency Press.
Cover design by Marie Triscari. Photograph by Eva Fernandez.
Front cover shows Irma Woods, Ernie Dingo and Trevor Jamieson.

Currency Press acknowledges the Traditional Owners of the Country on which we live and work. We pay our respects to all Aboriginal and Torres Strait Islander Elders, past and present.

Contents

Waltzing the Wilarra was first produced by Yirra Yaakin Theatre Company at Subiaco Arts Centre, Perth, on 5 February 2011 with the following cast:

OLD TOSS	Ernie Dingo
YOUNG HARRY	Jessica Clarke
MR MACK	Kelton Pell
MRS CRAY	Irma Woods
ELSA	Ursula Yovich
CHARLIE	Trevor Jamieson
JACK	Tim Solly
FAY	Alexandra Jones
ATHENA	Jessica Clarke

Director, Wesley Enoch
Music Director, Wayne Freer
Dramaturg, Sally Richardson
Set Designer, Jacob Nash
Costume Designer, Isaac Lummis
Lighting Designer, Trent Suidgeest
Sound Designer, Kingsley Reeve
Choreographer, Claudia Alessi
Musicians, Ric Eastman, Wayne Freer, David Milroy, Lucky Oceans, Bob Patient

CHARACTERS

OLD TOSS / SANDY BARR / DETECTIVE
Old Toss is a self-appointed elderly Aboriginal statesman and the purveyor of tainted wisdom to his sidekick Young Harry. He is adept in colloquialisms that are usually a few crumbs short of a biscuit.

MR MACK
Mr Mack is the Aboriginal Master of ceremonies at the club. He demands respect from the patrons and keeps an eye out for any troublemakers. He fancies himself as a bit of a comedian and a singer.

CHARLIE RUNAWAY / OLD CHARLIE
Charlie is one of the main Aboriginal performers at the club and quite the eligible young bachelor. He takes pride in his appearance and makes the most of his second-hand clothes.

MRS CRAY / SPIRIT MRS CRAY
Mrs Cray is an Aboriginal nanny and housemaid by day and club organiser by night. The club is the bright light in Mrs Cray's ordinary life.

ELSA / OLD ELSA
Elsa is Mrs Cray's daughter and the headline act at the club. Her clothes are often made of curtains but she holds her own in anything she wears.

JACK / SPIRIT JACK
Jack is a white returned soldier. He is married to Elsa and suffers from post-traumatic stress.

FAY GRIVER / OLD FAY
Fay is a young white woman from a well-to-do family. Mrs Cray is her Nanny.

ATHENA / YOUNG HARRY / LEVINIA TEMPLETON
Athena is the granddaughter of Fay and has an interest in contemporary political movements and has taken on the reconciliation mantle.

This book went to press before the end of rehearsals, and may differ from the play as performed.

ACT ONE

Lighting effects of water, stars and the Wilarra moon overhead.

OLD CHARLIE *stands centre stage.*

Musical underscore: 'Waltzing the Wilarra'.

OLD CHARLIE: I stood with my mother, beneath the paperbarks, at the edge of the Marble Bar pool. The night was so still, the stars floated on the water. She told me, 'Walk up to your chest and don't make any noise'. I could hear voices echoing along the edge of the pool. I looked across the water and the stars and the Wilarra moon shone so brightly, I couldn't tell where the night sky ended and the pool begun. I was standing in the universe... in the womb... of my new mother.

> *Old-style red curtains are drawn across the stage in front of* OLD CHARLIE.
>
> *A marching band enters.*
>
> *Two vaudeville tramps dance behind the band.*
>
> *The band exits behind the curtain.*
>
> YOUNG HARRY *goes to follow but is stopped by* OLD TOSS.

OLD TOSS: Hold your corsets, Young Harry!

YOUNG HARRY: Fair whip of the crack, Old Toss! What's the go?

OLD TOSS: It's after six o'clock!

YOUNG HARRY: That's nothing to gum ya flaps about!

OLD TOSS: When the hands are lined up, I can't cross the Caucasian Chalk Circle. So cop that, Young Harry!

YOUNG HARRY: The Caucasian Chalk Circle?

OLD TOSS: And unless I'm mistaken I sees no Cork or Asian in me.

YOUNG HARRY: Who's responsible for this travellers' tea, Old Toss?!

OLD TOSS: The Royal Order of the Boot!

YOUNG HARRY: The Royal Order of the Boot?

> YOUNG HARRY *stands to attention and blows a fanfare on a toy trumpet.* OLD TOSS *pulls out a scroll.*

OLD TOSS: [*reading*] 'Therefore, thereby and thus far, the city of Perth has been declared a prohibited area under Section Thirty-Nine of the Aborigines Act of 1905.' So cop that, Young Harry!

YOUNG HARRY: Sez who, Old Toss?

OLD TOSS: Why, Mr Neville of course!

YOUNG HARRY: Well, flog me chops! Who's he?

OLD TOSS: The King made him Protector of Aborigines from white people, and white people from Aborigines! We all need protecting around here, Young Harry.

YOUNG HARRY: God save the King!

> YOUNG HARRY *blows a fanfare.*

OLD TOSS: [*reading*] 'By the Royal Order of the Boot, therefore, thereby and thus far, Aborigines found loitering, littering, laughing, leaping or lolly-popping will be accosted and arrested if they cannot explain their presence in the city.'

YOUNG HARRY: Flatten me feet and call me a duck!

OLD TOSS: Quack! Quack! Young Harry! I has to be out of the city by six o'clock and look out if I get caught.

YOUNG HARRY: Don't worry, Old Toss. I'm white so you can be my black shadow.

OLD TOSS: Fair suck of the old sovereign, Young Harry! You can't mix black and white.

YOUNG HARRY: Hmmm! Sounds like a bit of a grey area to me.

OLD TOSS: We'd be arrested for consorting!

YOUNG HARRY: By my gummy mud boots! We's can't go courting if there's no resorting to consorting.

OLD TOSS: Cop this, Young Harry. There's one place we can go.

YOUNG HARRY: Spill the baked beans on me, Old Toss?

> *The band's big drum can be heard from offstage.*

OLD TOSS: Can you hear that, Young Harry?

YOUNG HARRY: It's rattling the bales off me wickets!

OLD TOSS: You in for a squiz, Young Harry?

YOUNG HARRY: If you're in for a penny, I'm in for a throo-pence!

> *The curtain opens to reveal the club. There are a few chairs and a table with an urn for tea and biscuits. Centre stage is the band.*

OLD TOSS: People pour into city from country towns and camps along the railway. They get here *any* way they can. On the top of wheat trains, on the back of trucks, even on the back of someone else's back.

YOUNG HARRY: I detect a glimmer in ya Zimmer, Old Toss!

OLD TOSS: *Luna azure*! Young Harry! The proverbial blue moon, and once in a blue moon we's gets to have some fun!

MR MACK *moves to the microphone and sings.*

'LITTLE BIRDY'

MR MACK: [*sung*]
    Choo! Choo! Sugar, I have to confess,
    There's a bird on my shoulder that's building a nest.
    Perch, little birdie, on top of my head,
    Singing in the morning till I get out of bed.
    But when the night-time comes,
    Me and little birdie like to have a little fun.

CHORUS:
    The stage is set for a party tonight,
    The stage is set for a party tonight,
    The stage is set for a party tonight,
    Look to the left,
    Look to the right,
    The stage is set for a party tonight.

MR MACK:
    Little birdy doing what a birdy gotta do,
    Djitty djitty wagging all his tail feathers too,
    Wardung in the corner as the *coolbardi* sings,
    Every birdy dancing and a shaking their wings.

    Repeat chorus.

Welcome! Welcome and welcome! We have a fine line-up of—

MRS CRAY *enters.*

MRS CRAY: Excuse me, Mr Mack!

MR MACK: Yes, Mrs Cray.

MRS CRAY: I'm not happy!

MR MACK: And why not?

MRS CRAY: The girls can't tell who the single mans are?

MR MACK: Well, that's easy. They're the ones that are still smiling!

> [*Sung*] Every little birdie needs another birdie too,
> One little birdie in a nest won't do,
> Two little birdies dancin' on the wall,
> Little birdies jigger bugging, havin' a ball.
> And when that night-time comes,
> Me and little birdie like to have a little fun.

> *Repeat chorus.*

> *The song ends.*

> *Patrons clap and whistle.*

Thank you! Thank you! And thank you! Tonight we have a fine line-up of performers accompanied by none other than Mr Wallace and the Fabulous Swing Quartet.

> *Drum roll.*

> *Patrons clap and whistle.*

MRS CRAY: We ask for a small donation to cover the cost of tea and biscuits, and for the enjoyment of others, please conduct yourself in a sober and orderly manner.

MR MACK: That means no getting pissed or fighting! And now, ladies and gentlemans, how about a big hand for Charlie Runaway and... the singer you've all come to see... Elsa Hammond!

> *Musical intro: 'I've Got Eyes'*

> ELSA *and* CHARLIE *sing.*

'I'VE GOT EYES'

ELSA & CHARLIE: [*sung*]
> I've got eyes for someone,
> I've got eyes for no-one,
> Except the man with the spurs,
> Buckle, hat and curls,
> A cowgirl in love,
> I've got a coat and a flash hat,
> This country girl don't care about that,
> I want the man with the spurs,

Buckle, hat and curls,
A cowgirl in love.

CHORUS:

We can go driving in my new car,
I'd rather be camping beneath the stars,
We can park and listen to the radio,
I'd rather be riding in a rodeo.

Repeat verse.

Instrumental.

Repeat chorus.

Repeat verse.

JACK *enters.*

He staggers past the dancers and slumps at the front of the stage.

The song ends.

Patrons clap.

JACK: I got a song!

MR MACK: How about a big hand for Elsa Hammond! What a star! And, Charlie, you'd better buy a horse, you might have more luck with the ladies.

JACK: Are you deaf or something!

MR MACK: That's right, everybody! You heard Mrs Cray, a *sober* and *orderly* manner!

JACK: I wanna sing a song!

MR MACK: And good for you, Jack. Put your name on the performers' list at the side of the stage. And now, ladies and—

JACK: Bugger the list!

MR MACK: Not now!

JACK *sings.*

'DESERT RATS'

JACK: [*sung*]

In one hand we held a rifle,
With the enemy at our gates,
In the other was a shovel,
To bury all our mates.

Patrons murmur.

MR MACK: Settle down! Settle down!

JACK: [*sung*]
> The cowards sat at home,
> With white feathers in their hats,
> While we starved and fought in Tobruk,
> God save the Desert Rats!

Patrons clap politely.

MR MACK: Thank you, Jack, for that heartfelt song.

ELSA *stands with* JACK.

JACK: I wanna go home.

ELSA: Not yet, Jack, let's have a bit of fun!

JACK: We can have fun at home!

ELSA: Tonight's our special night.

JACK: Then let's spend it by ourselves!

MR MACK: Great song, Elsa. You're certainly pulling a crowd.

ELSA: Thank you, Mr Mack.

MR MACK: I was thinking next week you and Charlie could do an extra—

JACK: Ya can find someone else, she's taking a break!

MR MACK: Is everything okay?

ELSA: It's our wedding anniversary.

MR MACK: Been celebrating, hey Jack?

JACK: Too right!

MR MACK: What's in the bottle?

ELSA: Medication.

MR MACK: Ya shouldn't mix it with beer.

JACK: I'm mixing it with whiskey!

ELSA: He's only joking.

MR MACK: Just remember, the police are keeping an eye on this place.

JACK: Hey, I'm not a blackfella, I can drink where I want!

MR MACK: Not here you can't, and the next time you wanna sing, put your name on the list, happy anniversary.

MR MACK *leaves.*

JACK: Prick!

ELSA: No, Jack! He's doing a good job running the club.

JACK: Fuck him, ya not singing here anymore.
ELSA: Don't swear! You used to like me singing.
JACK: When you was singing with me, not Charlie.
ELSA: We can sing together again.
JACK: You mean that?
ELSA: Of course I do, Charlie's just filling in till you get better.
JACK: You don't need him.
ELSA: Stop being jealous.
JACK: I'm not jealous!
ELSA: You're the one who asked him to take over when you signed up.
JACK: It was our act, not his.
ELSA: And it will be. Remember our song?

She takes his hands and sings.

> [*Sung*] I'm in love with a soldier boy,
> He's been redeployed,
> To protect my heart from all other boys,
> My wartime honey.

JACK:
> My sugar bunny.

ELSA:
> My wartime honey and me.

JACK: That's our song, aye?
ELSA: Our special song. One day we'll sing it together, just like we used to before the war.
JACK: I nearly forgot, I didn't wrap it, but I hope you like it.

JACK takes a present from his pocket.

ELSA: A ribbon.
JACK: It's not much.
ELSA: It's pretty. Thank you.

She gives him a kiss on the cheek.

MRS CRAY approaches with a cup of tea.

Look what Jack gave me, Mum, for our anniversary.
MRS CRAY: That's lovely.
ELSA: Could you tie it for me?
MRS CRAY: Maybe later. Here ya go, Jack, a nice hot cuppa.

JACK *stands and accidently knocks the tea out of* MRS CRAY *'s hand.*

MR MACK: Jeez, what now! I've had enough of you!

CHARLIE: It's alright, Mr Mack. Nothing to worry about, just a little accident!

MR MACK: One more little accident and he's out of here!

FAY: Patrons should behave. In a sober and—

JACK: Fuck off, Fay! Charlie! Give me a smoke!

CHARLIE *looks for a smoke in his coat.* FAY *confronts* ELSA.

FAY: Such language! I think you should take him home.

ELSA: When we're ready!

FAY: Hopefully, soon! You know the rules!

CHARLIE: Fay! Stay out of it.

FAY: And you should too. Come on, I've got lots to tell you about Daddy's birthday.

CHARLIE: Let's have a smoke outside.

FAY: Daddy would really like you, Charles.

CHARLIE: Nothin' like a bit of fresh air, aye soldier!

CHARLIE *grabs* JACK *'s arm.* JACK *pulls away. They face each other.*

JACK: I am a soldier. Just remember that!

CHARLIE: You were decommissioned three years ago.

JACK: Once a soldier, always a soldier!

JACK *staggers.*

CHARLIE: Let's go before you fall on your ugly face.

JACK: God save the Desert Rats!

JACK *and* CHARLIE *exit.*

FAY: Don't take too long, Charles, you'll miss out on the foxtrot! I'll get Nanny to bring you some tea and biscuits!

MRS CRAY: Jack seems a little… under the weather.

ELSA: He's been celebrating.

MRS CRAY: How about a cuppa?

ELSA: You don't have to wait on me.

MRS CRAY: If you need a ride home I can…

ELSA: And what? Get Fay to drive me. I'm not a charity case like you.

FAY: I hope Charles can settle him down.

MRS CRAY: He'll be alright.

FAY: He should be home sleeping it off.

ELSA: Stay out of it!

MRS CRAY: She's only trying to help.

ELSA: I don't need her help or yours.

FAY: Come on, Nanny, let's make them a cup of tea.

MRS CRAY: Fay, I want to talk to Elsa alone for a while.

FAY: Nanny?

ELSA: You heard her, you don't belong here, go home!

MRS CRAY: Elsa! That's not what I meant, Fay's welcome here.

ELSA: Fine, but she doesn't need a nanny, *here*!

MRS CRAY: It's just a name.

ELSA: Then come and live with me and Jack.

MRS CRAY: Listen, Elsa, this is not the place to be talking about—

ELSA: You're my mother not hers. I need you!

MRS CRAY: It's not that I don't want—

FAY: Nanny lives with our family and that's that!

MRS CRAY: Fay! Be quiet!

FAY: I'm only telling the truth!

> ELSA *fronts* FAY.

ELSA: You come here again, and I swear, I'll knock you legs up!

> ELSA *storms off.*

MRS CRAY: Elsa!

FAY: What did I say, Nanny?

MRS CRAY: Next time, for God's sake keep your mouth shut!

FAY: Humph!

MRS CRAY: Now, go make *me* a cuppa tea!

FAY: But Nanny?

MRS CRAY: Now!

FAY: Huh!

> MR MACK *is on stage.*

MR MACK: Okay, everybody! Next week we're holding a competition for the most original bathing suit.

> *Patrons clap and whistle.*

So, ladies, get sewing and, men, get polishing ya glasses! In the mean-time put your hands together for, Elsa Hammond!

> *Musical intro: 'Shadow Heart'.*

ELSA: Tonight is me and Jack's first wedding anniversary and we...

ELSA *is overwhelmed.*

MR MACK: C'mon, give 'em a clap!

Patrons clap.

We owe men like Jack a great deal, so come on, everybody! Stop wearing out the chairs and get on the dance floor!

ELSA *sings.*

'SHADOW HEART'

ELSA: [*sung*]
> There's a heart with a shadow tonight,
> That man of mine, he just don't treat me right,
> When he's drinking I'm home thinking,
> When he's smoking I'm sitting moping.
> There's a heart with a shadow tonight.
>
> I used to have a man with loving arms,
> Now he's found another woman with his charms,
> Instead of kissing he's gone missing,
> Instead of hugging he's out loving,
> There's a heart with a shadow tonight,
> Yes, there's a heart with a shadow tonight.

The song ends.

Outside the club JACK *takes a bottle from his coat and swigs.*

CHARLIE: Put it away; don't give the coppers an excuse.

JACK: Present from Hollywood Hospital!

JACK *throws the bottle to* CHARLIE *who takes a sniff.*

CHARLIE: Bloody hell! That can't be good for ya!

JACK: Supposed to settle me nerves. Works better if I mix it with this.

JACK *reveals a hip flask.* CHARLIE *hands back the bottle.*

CHARLIE: Ya like our song?

JACK: Ya like mine?

CHARLIE: I've had enough of war songs.

JACK: Is that so?

CHARLIE: The war's over.

JACK: Hah! It was never on for you in the first place!

CHARLIE: You're a civilian now.

JACK: Too right, and that's why I don't want you singing with her anymore.

CHARLIE: It's just a bit of fun.

JACK: Not with my wife it ain't!

CHARLIE: That's not what I meant.

JACK: I seen the way ya look at her.

CHARLIE: Piss off!

JACK: When Dad took you in, he said we was brothers and that cuts both ways.

CHARLIE: There's nothin' between us.

JACK: And there never will be.

CHARLIE: If ya want me to stop singing with her, I will.

JACK: Good.

CHARLIE: But don't stop her from singing here.

JACK: Bugger the club. Here's to me and Elsa, and no more wars, big or small!

CHARLIE: No more wars.

> JACK *swigs.*

I wish I'd been there with ya.

JACK: They all say that. The cowards stayed at home with white feathers in their hats!

CHARLIE: You know I tried to sign up. It was only the rheumatic fever that stopped me.

JACK: You weren't the only coward to swallow soap.

CHARLIE: Piss off, Jack!

JACK: Give ya a bit of a heart flutter, aye? Aye?

CHARLIE: No good talking to ya when you're pissed.

JACK: You're a coward!

CHARLIE: Try telling me when ya sober, ya shit-stirring bastard!

JACK: It don't matter if I'm drunk or sober, you'll still be a coward!

CHARLIE: You're not so brave, what about the sack of puppies? Big war hero! I can still remember the look on your face when Dad asked ya to throw them off the jetty. Can't feed em' all, he said. I had to do it for ya. When I opened up the sack to make sure they was dead you spewed ya guts up.

JACK: Maybe Dad could see something in you I couldn't.

CHARLIE: I'm no coward.

JACK takes a swig.

JACK: It was simpler when we was kids, playing down the river. Jellyfish fights, rafts made out of forty-fours. Wrestle in the sand till one of us went over the line.

CHARLIE: I don't think I ever won a fight. But I reckon I can take ya now!

He jokingly grabs JACK around the neck.

He slams him into the turnbuckle, but he recovers and grips him in the sleeper hold. One! Two!

JACK snores.

Three!

He releases JACK.

JACK: Whew! Don't remember that hold.

CHARLIE: That's 'cause you was asleep.

JACK laughs.

We were brothers, Jack, and we still are. Happy anniversary.

CHARLIE re-enters the hall.

A musical saw instrumental underscore.

FAY: Has he sobered up?

CHARLIE: He's alright.

FAY: No wonder he drinks, with Elsa as his wife.

CHARLIE: It's their anniversary!

FAY: Whoopy doo!

CHARLIE notices a cowgirl hat on the stage.

I think it would be more suitable if you sang with me. What if we formed our own duo?

CHARLIE: Elsa! Don't forget this [*the hat*].

ELSA: Thanks, Charlie.

CHARLIE: Jack's ready to call it a night.

FAY: Finally you can dance with me. Come on.

CHARLIE: In a minute.

FAY: Don't be too long. We've wasted enough time already.

　　FAY *leaves.*

ELSA: Looks like you're in for a good night.

CHARLIE: It's not like that, we're just dance partners.

ELSA: Ya dancing with fire.

CHARLIE: It's nothing.

ELSA: Hmmm. I gotta go, but next time we'll get through the whole act.

CHARLIE: Listen, Elsa, Jack's getting funny about us singing together.

ELSA: He's just a little jealous, that's all.

CHARLIE: Best you sing with him.

ELSA: Maybe later when he's better, but not now.

CHARLIE: It's only causing trouble.

ELSA: He'll be fine once he sobers up.

CHARLIE: You used to sing with him before, and besides, you're the star.

ELSA: Shush, Charlie! Tomorrow he won't even remember what he said.

CHARLIE: I'm sorry. It's for the best.

　　He gently touches her shoulder and she flinches with pain.

　　He grabs her arm and raises her sleeve to reveal bruising.

ELSA: Don't!

CHARLIE: What the hell is this?

ELSA: It's nothing.

CHARLIE: Bullshit it's nothing.

　　He turns her head to the side to check for bruising. ELSA *shies away.*

ELSA: He'll get over it.

CHARLIE: You don't have to put up with this.

ELSA: I'm not going back to living in the camps!

CHARLIE: Your mum can get you a job. She knows lots of rich families.

ELSA: I want my own home and my own family.

CHARLIE: It won't stop, you know.

ELSA: Once we have children he'll be right.

CHARLIE: That won't change things!

ELSA: I love him, and he loves me, that's all that matters!

CHARLIE: He doesn't love you! You're only medicine for him!

ELSA: Just keep ya mouth shut!

CHARLIE: At least tell your mother what's going on.

ELSA: I'm nothing to her. While she was nursing Fay I was in a children's home. Even now, she doesn't want me. Jack's my life, he's all I've got, so back off!

FAY *and* MRS CRAY *approach.*

MRS CRAY: I've wrapped some biscuits for Jack.

FAY: What a nice dress your wearing, Elsa. Oh, Nanny, aren't those the curtains we threw out?

CHARLIE: Some women look good in anything, Fay.

FAY: Maybe I should have worn a tablecloth.

MRS CRAY: [*to* ELSA] Do you need a ride home?

FAY: Charles and I can drop you off. Then we can park and listen to the radio.

ELSA: We'll find our own way home.

CHARLIE: You should go with her, Mrs Cray.

FAY: Sorry, Charles, but it's Daddy's birthday tomorrow and she has to be up bright and early to fix Daddy's breakfast.

CHARLIE: Just for tonight.

MRS CRAY: I'm sure you can fix Oscar his breakfast.

FAY: No-one cooks bacon like you, Nanny!

ELSA: I'll be fine! Wouldn't want to break up a happy family.

ELSA *storms off.*

MRS CRAY: Elsa!

FAY: Such a temper!

MRS CRAY: Sometimes, Fay, you need to pull back on your words.

FAY: Humph! Biscuit, Charles?

Musical intro: 'Tangled Tango' (a band song).

ELSA *and* JACK *dance their own dysfunctional tango outside the club.* CHARLIE *sets* FAY *on fire with his dance.*

'TANGLED TANGO'

BAND: [*sung*]
    When lovers dance the tangled tango,
    They twist and turn at every angle,
    Hearts burning with wild desire,
    Dancing with fire.

> Broken hearts get flung together,
> Twisted minds of steamy pleasure
> As the dance goes to the wire,
> Dancing with fire.

CHORUS:
> Gentle hand upon the waist,
> Other grips with a firm embrace,
> Lips so close you can almost taste,
> The final act, the lovers' pact,
> The horizontal aphrodisiac.

BAND:
> Tango danced and hearts are pounding,
> The heavy breath of passions mounting,
> A stolen glance with longing eyes,
> Dancing with fire.
> The final thrust and nothings spoken,
> The tango's spell remains unbroken,
> Perfume of pure delight,
> Dancing with fire.

Repeat chorus.

The song ends.

Curtains are drawn.

Transition to another night.

OLD TOSS *and* YOUNG HARRY *enter.*

OLD TOSS: Cop this, Young Harry! There's nothing better than a bathing suit competition.

YOUNG HARRY: And there's nothing better than dressing to the nines!

OLD TOSS: The only problem is, I'm only dressed to the ones and twos.

YOUNG HARRY: There must be something to make you look extinguished!

OLD TOSS: I've got it… dignity!

YOUNG HARRY: Dignity?

OLD TOSS: I can polish me boots!

YOUNG HARRY: Too right, Old Toss!

OLD TOSS: Polish me teeth!

YOUNG HARRY: Too right, Old Toss!

OLD TOSS: And even polish me polish!

YOUNG HARRY: Too right, old Toss! All men were created equal, and you, as a Terra Nullian, demand the right to be equalised, dignified and polished!

OLD TOSS: Too left, Young Harry! Techa-nickally speaking, I don't exist. I'm just a pigment of the imagined nation.

YOUNG HARRY *blows his trumpet.*

By the Royal Order of the Boot! Therefore, thereby and thus far, dignity is reserved only for citizens of Australia not Terra Nullians.

YOUNG HARRY: Well, poke me in the pie with a blunt pick! That counts you out, Old Toss. What about polishing your boots?

YOUNG HARRY *blows his trumpet.*

OLD TOSS: By the Royal Order of the Boot, no polished boots for Terra Nullians unless applied to the backside by a police officer.

YOUNG HARRY: Fair cut of the umbilical sword, Old Toss! What about wearing hand-me-downs?

YOUNG HARRY *blows his trumpet.*

OLD TOSS: By the Royal Order of the Boot, Terra Nullians will be subject to the removal of their children and property so that nothing can be handed down and there'll be no-one to hand down to. So cop that, Young Harry!

YOUNG HARRY: I guess you're gonna have to go to the bathing suit competition as a Terra Nullian, vaudevillian trampoline!

OLD TOSS: Don't count ya chickens with a hatchet, Young Harry! [*He opens his coat to reveal he's wearing a golden bathing suit.*] Whadda ya reckon?

YOUNG HARRY: I think you might be in with a trance, Old Toss. But just remember, if you don't win, at least you didn't come first.

OLD TOSS: Too right, Young Harry!

The big band drum can be heard playing offstage.

Curtains open to reveal the night of the bathing suit competition.

Band outro plays.

MR MACK: Welcome! Welcome! And welcome! Mr Wallace and the Fabulous Swing Quartet have just had a request, but they're gonna keep playing anyway!

Drum: Boom boom.

MRS CRAY: You know, Mr Mack, I touched my nose the other day and the pain was terrible.

MR MACK: Really?

MRS CRAY: In fact everything I touched hurt so badly I went to the doctor.

MR MACK: And what did he say?

MRS CRAY: I had a broken finger!

Drum: Boom boom.

MR MACK: Thank you for supporting the bathing suit competition and the contestants for their supports too!

Musical outro plays.

MR MACK *and* MRS CRAY *leave the stage.*

CHARLIE *approaches* MRS CRAY.

CHARLIE: Is Elsa coming?

MRS CRAY: I don't know.

CHARLIE: Playing the good wife, I suppose.

MRS CRAY: And what's wrong with that?

CHARLIE: Jack's not exactly the good husband.

MRS CRAY: Every marriage has its ups and downs.

CHARLIE: One more thing to keep quiet about, aye?

MRS CRAY: What are you talking about?

CHARLIE: She'd better leave him while she still can.

MRS CRAY: You stay out of their business.

CHARLIE: At least she wouldn't cop a flogging from me!

MRS CRAY: What?

MR MACK: Is everything alright?

MRS CRAY: She's never said anything to me, so don't you dare stir up trouble!

MRS CRAY *storms off.*

MR MACK: Thanks for being the judge tonight, Charlie.

CHARLIE: I'm sorry, Mr Mack, I gotta go.

MR MACK: Don't be silly, you're a single man judging a bathing suit competition. You couldn't ask for more than that.

CHARLIE: I'm not up for it.

MR MACK: How about if we move the competition forward?

CHARLIE: Alright, I won't let you down.

MR MACK: Just a word of advice. Let Jack and Elsa sort their own business out.

> MR MACK *leaves.*

FAY: I wouldn't count on her turning up.

CHARLIE: He can't keep her home forever.

FAY: That's if she's at home.

CHARLIE: Where else would she be?

FAY: I really shouldn't be talking to the judge.

CHARLIE: What's going on?

FAY: I just hope the *judge* pays as much attention to my swimsuit as he does to Elsa's whereabouts.

CHARLIE: What's going on?

FAY: It's none of our business.

CHARLIE: Is she crook?

FAY: You could say that.

CHARLIE: Tell me!

FAY: She's been in hospital for the past few days.

CHARLIE: What?

FAY: Jack called me the other night. He was in a bad way and asked me to drive her to the hospital.

CHARLIE: How bad is she?

FAY: She lost… she'll be alright.

CHARLIE: Bastard!

FAY: She's a married woman, till death do they part!

CHARLIE: Not if I can help it.

> FAY *grabs his arm.*

FAY: Charles, there are other women, single women, women who would cherish y… you have to forget about Elsa and open your eyes, just a little.

CHARLIE: My eyes are open.

FAY: Can't you see the world has changed, everything is possible.

> CHARLIE *pulls away.*

CHARLIE: I don't care about the world, I only care about—

FAY: I know you love her, but she doesn't love you!

Drum roll.

MRS CRAY *is on stage with* MR MACK.

MR MACK: Ladies and gentlemans, there's been a change of program. The swimsuit competition for nine o'clock has been cancelled.

Patrons boo.

It's now at eight o'clock.

Patrons cheer.

But it's only for men.

Patrons boo.

To look at!

Patrons cheer.

MRS CRAY: Would all the contestants please make their way to the side of the stage?

MR MACK: Our judge for tonight is none other than the dashing, the debonair... Mr Charlie Runaway!

Drum roll.

CHARLIE *takes a reluctant bow.*

MRS CRAY: The girls will be judged on the following criteria: bathing suit originality, poise and talent.

OLD TOSS: What about their legs?!

MR MACK: Ladies and gentlemen! Our first contestant for tonight is Miss Levinia Templeton.

Parade music.

Levinia lives in Bassendean and enjoys swimming, digging for worms to catch cobbler, cooking cobbler and eating cobbler. Let's have a big hand for Miss Cobbl... Miss Levinia Templeton!

OLD TOSS: Show us ya cobblers!

The parade music ends.

MR MACK: And what song have you chosen?

LEVINIA: It's one of my own compositions called... 'In the Deep Blue Sea'.

Musical intro: 'Deep Blue Sea'.

'DEEP BLUE SEA'

> [*Sung*] Way down, down! Way down, down!
> Digging for worms in the slippery mud,
> I just can't seem to get enough,
> Gonna have to put my swimsuit on,
> And find out where the cobbler's gone.
>
> Way down, down! Way down, down!
> Way down, down in the deep blue sea,
> The big fat cobblers hiding from me,
> Dead or alive, dead or alive,
> Into the ocean I will dive.
>
> Way down, down! Way down, down!
> Swimming down, down in the deep blue sea,
> The big fat cobbler's hiding in the weed,
> I grab him carefully with my hand,
> Tonight he'll be cooking in the frying in the pan.

Ssssssssss!

> *Patrons clap politely.*

MR MACK: Well done, Miss Levinia Templeton! There's something very fishy about that song.

OLD TOSS: Left me feeling like a stunned mullet!

MR MACK: Our next contestant is Miss Fay Griver.

> *Parade music.*

Miss Fay lives in Claremont and her hobbies include shopping, shopping and, you guessed it, shopping. Fay does voluntary work for the Red Cross and recently deferred her studies in Archaeology.

> *The parade music ends.*

Archaeology, hey? Well, there's a few fossils in the audience tonight! And what have you *dug* up for us?

FAY: A little rumba called 'Misty Moon'.

> *Musical intro: 'Misty Moon'.*

> FAY *dances seductively up to* CHARLIE, *who is embarrassed.*

'MISTY MOON'

> [*Sung*] Setting sun, setting sun,

Don't cast your shadow on me.
Setting sun, setting sun,
Don't cast your shadow on me.
'Cause I'm looking for a man
And it's way too dark to see.

Misty moon, misty moon,
Point to where my love could be.
Misty moon, misty moon,
Point to where my love could be.
When the sun comes up tomorrow
He'll be loving only me.

Evening star, evening star,
Can you give me some advice?
Evening star, evening star,
Can you give me some advice?
Should I keep on loving him?
Or start a brand new life?
Should I keep on loving him?
Or start a brand new life?

As the song ends, FAY *places the scarf around* CHARLIE*'s neck.*

Patrons clap and whistle.

MR MACK: I don't think you'll need a scarf tonight, Charlie, it's getting pretty hot in here!

CHARLIE *is embarrassed and tucks the scarf into his pocket.*

JACK *and* ELSA *enter.*

And now, ladies and gentlemans, our third contestant is Miss Sandy Barr.

Parade music.

SANDY*'s swimsuit has various military overtones to it.*

MR MACK: Miss Sandy's hobbies include high jump, long jump and hurdles. Her swimsuit is a tribute to all Aboriginal soldiers.

The parade music ends.

And what song have you chosen?

SANDY: I've penned a war poem in honour of our Aboriginal soldiers called 'Dear Mother England'.

Tuba underscore.

'DEAR MOTHER ENGLAND'

> [*Sung*] When the fighting was at its fiercest
> And the battlefield was black,
> There was a promise that cheered you on,
> You'll get a job when you get back!

Patrons react.

> You were not professional soldiers,
> Fighting was not your game,
> You were only peaceful blacks
> Who fought hard just the same.

Patrons react.

> You sacrificed your wives and kids
> Just to do your bit,
> But now you're back the door is closed
> To make a go of it.

Patrons react.

> Dear Mother England,
> You think you know a lot,
> Holding onto the Commonwealth
> And talking tommyrot.

> Mother England's bosoms
> Swelling up with pride,
> From all the blacks in Australia,
> Your arse is much too wide!

SANDY *bends over to reveal a Union Jack on her backside.*

Patrons go wild.

JACK *smashes a chair on the dance floor.*

JACK: You're not the only bastards who got done over!

MR MACK: Settle down, Jack!

JACK: Half you blacks wouldn't take a job if it was thrown at ya!

ELSA: Sit down. Please sit down.

CHARLIE: Come on, you're ruining the night!

JACK: Fuck off, Charlie! You never went to war, ya coward!

ELSA: Jack!

CHARLIE: Who's a coward?! C'mon, you tell me who's the coward!

JACK: Rheumatic fever, my arse! You soap-swallowing bastard!

CHARLIE: You're the coward, ya wife-beating prick!

> CHARLIE *throws a punch. Tables are upturned.* JACK *is pushed back and slumps into a chair.* OLD TOSS *places a large badge on his coat and walks around blowing a whistle until the crowd subdues. Band members become police.*

DETECTIVE: Settle down! Settle down or we'll shut this place once and for all! Who's in charge?

MR MACK: I am, Detective.

DETECTIVE: I'm not against you running this club, but we've received a complaint.

MR MACK: You got here pretty quick.

CHARLIE: Parked right outside the hall.

FAY: Quiet, Charles.

MR MACK: There's no trouble here, just a little scuffle that's all.

DETECTIVE: Bit of drinking going on?

MR MACK: No grog here.

MRS CRAY: Just tea and biscuits.

> DETECTIVE *notices* JACK *slumped in the chair.*

DETECTIVE: What about whitey over there? Looks pissed to me.

MR MACK: He's on medication.

DETECTIVE: Medication, hey? Could do with some of that myself. [*He finds* JACK'*s medicine and sniffs the bottle.*] The only thing worse than uppity blacks is the white folk who hang around them.

> *The* DETECTIVE *pours the medicine over* JACK. JACK *spits in the* DETECTIVE'*s face.*

Bastard!

ELSA: He's not well!

DETECTIVE: And who are you?

ELSA: I'm his wife.

DETECTIVE: Papers!

> ELSA *hands the* DETECTIVE *papers.*

You're wasting your time with him. You could be making good money down on Roe Street instead of giving it away for free.

ELSA: I'm a married woman.

DETECTIVE: Maybe you should come to the station and keep me company while he sleeps it off.

ELSA: We haven't done anything, we're not criminals!

JACK *mumbles.*

JACK: Criminals.

DETECTIVE: What's that, shithead?

JACK: I said. We're all fucking criminals! Hey, Charlie?

CHARLIE: Shut up, Jack!

JACK: Every damn one of us!

ELSA: He's not thinking straight, Detective. I'll take him home.

ELSA *goes to leave but the* DETECTIVE *grabs her by the arm.*

DETECTIVE: Stay where you are.

ELSA *bows her head.* JACK *circles the* DETECTIVE *and* ELSA.

Musical intro: 'Criminal Love'.

JACK: You must have seen a lot of loving, Detective, the kitchen knife in the husband's heart, the suicide note under the pill bottle, cut-throat razor by the bath? I'm sure you've seen it all. We're all criminals when it comes to love.

JACK *sings.*

'CRIMINAL LOVE'

> [*Sung*] Love is a criminal, it'll steal your heart then hide it away,
> Love is a vandal, it'll ruin your life and leave you maimed,
> Love is an arsonist of the very worst crime,
> Lovers get burnt time after time,
> And I've got that criminal, arsonist mind, so lock me away.
>
> Put the handcuffs on and tighten the noose,
> When it comes to love I've been a little loose,
> Strap me in tight to the electric chair,
> Turn up the volts till it burns my hair.
> I've had a lethal injection of love all my life,
> It's finally kicked in on this lonely night,
> I've got that criminal, arsonist mind, so lock me away.

DETECTIVE: These are not sort of people you should be mixing with, Miss... Miss?

FAY: Fay Griver, of the Claremont Grivers.

The DETECTIVE *writes her name in his book.*

DETECTIVE: You should know better.

The song continues.

JACK: [*sung*]
> Bury me 'neath the old pine tree,
> My wounds are carved in more hearts than you can see,
> Nail the lid on my coffin nice and tight,
> No more wandering on those whiskey-fuelled nights,
> Don't hold back on my headstone epitaph,
> Here lies a man that took lovin' too far.
> He had a criminal, vandal, arsonist mind and we've locked him away,
> He had a criminal, vandal, arsonist mind and we've locked him away.

The music continues to the end of the scene.

DETECTIVE: You can sleep it off back at the station. [*He turns to* ELSA.] You're coming too. Wouldn't want to break up a happy family.

CHARLIE: He's my brother so you'd better take me as well! In fact we're all family here so why don't you take us all?

The DETECTIVE *grabs* CHARLIE *by the throat, as* ELSA *is spirited away by* MRS CRAY.

DETECTIVE: I don't know what your game is, sport, but keep it up and they'll find you floating in the Swan along with the rest of the sewerage. You can have a night in the lockup as well!

The DETECTIVE *exits.*

Transition to the lockup.

The music fades.

JACK *wakes up and looks around.*

JACK: Where are we?

CHARLIE: Go back to sleep.

JACK: What the fuck's going on?

CHARLIE: We're in the lockup.

JACK: What happened?

CHARLIE: You put us here, with your big mouth!

JACK: I don't re— Shit! Where's Elsa?

CHARLIE: Go to sleep!

JACK: Where is she?

CHARLIE: So now you care about her, well it's too bloody late.

JACK: Just tell me if she's alright!

CHARLIE: She's safe.

JACK: I remember now, we had a fight. You called me a wife beater!

CHARLIE: That's what you are.

JACK: Bullshit, Charlie! Who told you that, Fay?

CHARLIE: No-one told me, I seen the bruises for myself!

JACK: It was nothing, just an accident.

CHARLIE: And the hospital, that was an accident too?

JACK: It's not what you think.

CHARLIE: You gotta stop it, Jack, no more!

JACK: You love her, don't ya? You're just too gutless to admit it! When it comes to love, Charlie, you're still wearing that white feather!

CHARLIE: Let her go!

JACK: I shared my father with ya, I'm not gonna share my wife!

CHARLIE: Give her a chance!

JACK: I'll get better, so fuck off!

CHARLIE: I'm not gonna let you flog her to death!

JACK: I warned you to stay away but you gotta keep coming at me.

CHARLIE: Leave her!

JACK: I tried to tell ya but you won't leave us alone! You been with her, haven't you, while I was away? Hey? Hey?

CHARLIE: I've never been with her!

JACK: I'll kill you for what you done to me! I'll kill ya! I'll fucking kill ya!

He punches into CHARLIE *and grabs him by the throat.* JACK *slowly releases his grip.* CHARLIE *struggles to regain his breath.*

At night, I try to knock myself out with the medicine because I'm too scared to sleep. When I'm dreaming it's not her I see, she's just someone I'm fighting. I wake up and there she is, curled up on the floor crying. Tomorrow they're gonna let me out of here… [*speaking with terror in his eyes*] but I just want it to end.

JACK *looks pleadingly at* CHARLIE.

Musical underscore: 'Smoke and Mirrors'.

'SMOKE AND MIRRORS'

> [*Sung*] It's all just smoke and mirrors,
> So do what you have to do,
> When the smoky mists of time have cleared
> It's no reflection on you.
>
> Pull a hat out of a rabbit,
> Cut a magician's saw in half,
> Pull an ear out of a coin,
> Do the unthinkable with a scarf.
>
> Make the audience perform
> Whilst the clowns sit there and laugh,
> Let the lions crack the whip,
> Do the unthinkable with a scarf.
>
> It's all just smoke and mirrors,
> So do what you have to do,
> When the smoky mists of time have cleared
> It's no reflection on you.

JACK *slumps in the chair.*

Macabre patrons enter the jail.

PATRONS:

> Now you're balancing on a tightrope,
> It's getting slacker every step,
> You look down with a shiver,
> Someone's removed the net.
>
> The lions have been let loose,
> They're drooling for a feed,
> The clowns are swinging on the rope,
> There's butter on your feet.
>
> Then you make a giant leap,
> The audience all gasp,
> You slide on down the tent pole
> With your tiny little scarf.

Musical underscore as CHARLIE *takes the scarf from his pocket and stands over* JACK. JACK *opens his eyes and smiles. He squeezes* CHARLIE*'s hand then closes his eyes.*

> It's all just smoke and mirrors,
> So do what you have to do,
> When the smoky mists of time have cleared
> It's no reflection on you.

Musical underscore as all the patrons of the club do a macabre dance.

Transition back to the club.

The drummer is performing a solo.

MR MACK: Thank you! Thank you! And thank you! How about a big hand for Billy Stone? What a drummer!

Patrons clap and cheer.

MRS CRAY: It's Billy's birthday today.

MR MACK: I heard, he got a broken drum for a present.

MRS CRAY: Well, you can't beat that!

Drums: Boom boom.

I'm not happy with you, Mr Mack, setting me up with Old Henry last night. Our date was over in five minutes.

MR MACK: How come?

MRS CRAY: Would you go out with someone who was loudmouthed, with rotten teeth and bad breath?

MR MACK: No I wouldn't!

MRS CRAY: Well, neither would he!

The drummer plays a train shuffle.

Love can be a steam train full of steam…

MR MACK: Or a Puffing Billy out of puff!…

MRS CRAY: Or a runaway locomotive…

MR MACK: Hurtling through that tunnel of love…

MRS CRAY: You might not have a ticket…

MR MACK: For that train of love to stop…

MRS CRAY: But you can do the Wheatbelt Boogie…

MR MACK: By just jumping on top!

MR MACK *sings.*

During the song CHARLIE, ELSA *and* FAY *play out their own inner turmoil.*

'WHEATBELT BOOGIE'

[*Sung*] I've got a first-class ticket tonight,
Best view around,
Gotta make sure when the tunnel comes up,
I duck my head down,
On top of the wheat train,
Far as I can see,
Tonight I'm gonna do the Wheatbelt Boogie
With my chickadee.

Jump the train as it's slowin' down,
Miss the baton patrol,
Hit the ground with a smile on my face,
Thinking of my gal,
Straw in my hair,
Shoes full of wheat,
Tonight I'm gonna do the Wheatbelt Boogie
With my chickadee.

Instrumental.

My gal, she's wearing a brand new dress,
Curtains look real nice,
My shirts made out of a flour sack,
Got a hessian tie,
Cleaned my teeth with charcoal,
Hair slick as can be,
Tonight I'm gonna do the Wheatbelt Boogie
With my chickadee.

GIRLS:

Tonight I'm gonna do the Wheatbelt Boogie
With my man and me.

The song ends.

Patrons clap.

MR MACK: Elsa, on behalf of everyone here tonight, I'd like to express
our sorrow over the passing of Jack. We share your grief. Sometimes

we saw the rough side of him but inside he was a gentle caring man who wouldn't hurt a living soul. No-one's made for war, but duty called. To Jack!

PATRONS: To Jack!

MR MACK: I'm sure she could do with a helping hand, so dig deep, everyone!

> MR MACK *takes the hat around.*

FAY: Charles, I need to have a word with you in private.

CHARLIE: Not now, Fay.

FAY: It concerns Elsa.

CHARLIE: What is it?

FAY: We need to go outside.

MR MACK: Come on! Long pockets and short arms, you can do better than that! Alright! Who put the bottle top in the hat?

> FAY *and* CHARLIE *go outside.*

CHARLIE: What do you wanna tell me?

FAY: I have a proposition that I'd like you to consider.

CHARLIE: Go on.

FAY: I'm sure you are aware of my feelings for you, but I'm a realist. I know your heart is with Elsa. But sometimes we have to accept what we need, not what we want.

CHARLIE: Get on with it, Fay.

FAY: I've spoken to Daddy and I can get Elsa a weekly sum of money and possibly her own home, but this all depends on you being with me.

CHARLIE: What, like a couple?

FAY: I know Daddy will have trouble accepting that, but he'll come around. You may not love me, Charles, but Elsa doesn't love you either.

CHARLIE: Shame on you, thinking you can blackmail me into going with you!

FAY: Tell me what's worse, blackmail or murder.

> CHARLIE *is taken aback.*

Your friend, the detective, had my name in his book.

CHARLIE: So?

FAY: He told me you were in the same cell as Jack. They were unsure how he died.

CHARLIE: There's nothing to talk about.

FAY: Really? They asked me about the scarf and if I knew where it came from.

CHARLIE: What did ya tell them?

FAY: I told them I gave it to Jack. I lied for you, Charles.

CHARLIE: It wasn't like that. I…

FAY: Charles, will you be with me?

> CHARLIE *picks up some paperbark.*

> *Musical underscore.*

CHARLIE: When the police took me from my mother I was sitting under a paperbark tree waiting for her to come back. She'd given me some paperbark to put in my pocket. She told me to rub it if I was scared. It was soft like her skin. By the time I got to the Moore River Settlement it had turned to dust. I'm not gonna spend the rest of my life wondering. I'm sorry, Fay.

> CHARLIE *goes to exit.*

FAY: Charles, she's still getting over Jack, you need to give her some—

CHARLIE: I can do what I want.

FAY: Even if it means going to jail?

CHARLIE: Only if you open your mouth!

> MRS CRAY *approaches.*

> CHARLIE *goes to enter the hall.* FAY *tries to hold him back.*

FAY: No!

> CHARLIE *pushes* FAY.

CHARLIE: Back off!

MRS CRAY: What do you think you're doing? Are you alright, Fay?

> FAY *rubs her arm.*

[*To* CHARLIE] You stay away from my girls! You hear me!

> CHARLIE *enters the hall pursued by* MRS CRAY *and* FAY. MRS CRAY *gestures angrily towards* CHARLIE.

CHARLIE: Elsa, the union has offered me a job at the abattoirs.

ELSA: That's good, Charlie.

CHARLIE: They said I could have one of their worker's cottages if I'm married.

ELSA: Have you got someone in mind?

CHARLIE: I'll be earning good money, as good as a whitefella.

MR MACK: Outside, now!

CHARLIE: Elsa, will you marry me?

MR MACK: Are you mad? She's just lost her husband!

> MR MACK *grabs* CHARLIE *and moves him aside.* MRS CRAY *slaps* CHARLIE.

MRS CRAY: I told you to stay away from my girls!

CHARLIE: This is between me and Elsa.

MR MACK: Jack was like a brother to you!

MRS CRAY: What sort of a man are you?

MR MACK: That's enough!

> MR MACK *escorts* CHARLIE *to the door.*

ELSA: Charlie! Are you serious?

CHARLIE: I want you to marry me!

ELSA: I don't love you.

CHARLIE: I don't care.

MRS CRAY: You bastard!

> MRS CRAY *goes for* CHARLIE *but* MR MACK *stands between them.*

ELSA: Mum! Listen to me! Can't you see I've got nothing? All you have to do is be with me?

FAY: If you want Charlie, that's fine, but Nanny stays with me!

ELSA: Mum?

> MRS CRAY *doesn't respond.*

CHARLIE: Elsa, will you marry me?

> *Musical intro: 'Just One Word'.*

> JACK'S SPIRIT *enters the club dressed smartly in his uniform.* ELSA *takes the ribbon out of her pocket and sings.*

'JUST ONE WORD'

ELSA: [*sung*]
> Can there be so much meaning in just one word?
> Does it walk with your shadow from the moment of your birth?
> Can it float like a wave between your heart and the earth?
> Is it love? Is it love?

Can the word be the illness as well as the cure?
Can it whisper all night till the dark clouds turn pure?
Can the word be said in silence, can the word be just a look?
Is it love? Is it love?

Can a lover's touch pass through you and take hold of your
    heart?
Does it caress you so gently that it tears you apart?
Does it hold you on the edge by a shadow of a breath?
Is it love? Is it love?

Can it fade from your mind like the footprints on a beach?
Make your heart breathe a song as it sings away your sleep?
Ten green bottles smashed against the wall?
Is it love? Is it love?

The song ends.

Blackout.

END OF ACT ONE

ACT TWO

A dishevelled OLD TOSS *is sitting on a soapbox with an accordion.*
Musical intro: 'Yodelling Dingo'.

OLD TOSS *sings.*

'YODELLING DINGO'

OLD TOSS: [*sung*]
  The stockmen would talk around the campfire
  About the yodelling dingo dog,
  He'd yodel every night to the moonlight
  Longing for his only true love,
  Then one night his yodelling was answered
  By a yodelling dingo gal,
  Now they're as happy as can be 'neath the old gum tree
  With five yodelling puppies as well.

CHORUS:
  You're my lady,
  I'm your lady,
  You're my lady,
  I'm your lady,
  You're my lady,
  I'm your lady.

OLD TOSS:
  You're my yodelling dingo gal,
  Now the stockmans all know,
  His yodel lay-de-oh
  Is for his only true love,
  Now the stockmans all know,
  His yodel lay-de-oh
  Is for his only true love.

 Repeat chorus.

 A howl.

 The song ends.

According to the accordion no talent has ever rubbed off on me, and I'm not getting any older! As for *hidden* talent, I says to them that says that to me… ya did a bloody good job of hiding it. If ya happens to possess it, don't be possessed by it, or even worse, repossessed by it! I'm glad I ain't no Prince of Penmark! But if it's Spamlet you want! I'll shake the spear for a shilling! [*He stands on the soapbox.*] Huh! Hmmm! *Alas*, poor Your-Itch, I knew him… a lass? Even I knows, without one groin of talent, or a daddow of a shout, that Your-Itch was a lad, not a lass! [*He jumps off the soapbox.*] Talent is something you're bornded with and I don't sees none around. [*He lifts up the soapbox to reveal a football. He holds it up.*] According to the accordion! All the therefore, therebys and thusfars become terra nullius if a Terra Nullian can kick a footy. That's a career path, if ever I sordid one!… Hang on a minuet! [*He pulls a clown wig out of the footy.*] By the Royal Order of the Wig! A Terra Nullian can soar to unimaginable heights with deadly repartee, smiley teeth and the odd cubadee! But beware of snakes with ladders!

Underscore: 'Smoke and Mirrors'.

> [*Sung*] You can be a rooster one day or a feather duster the next,
> A minstrel amongst the tinsel or a jellyfish caught in the net,

He puts one foot on the soapbox.

> When you're standing on the stage, keep one foot on the ground,
> It's not as far to fall when they try to pull ya down.
> When you're Daniel in the lion's den and they're scratching for a fight,
> A tap-dance won't save you from their mighty bite.
> Be the clown that pulls the laughs and gets ta throw the pie,
> Not the one who forgot to duck and cops it in the eye.

The underscore ends.

Enough of this pie-in-the-eye talk! According to the accordion, there's only one talent that we's all needs to possess. Look after ya children and ya family and let life take care of the rest.

Musical outro: 'Yodelling Dingo'.

OLD TOSS *exits.*

A door slowly opens to reveal a shaft of light.

ATHENA *enters, a young pregnant woman, carrying a folder. She looks around the hall and flicks on a light switch.*

Lights come up.

The hall is fifty years on and in a state of disrepair. A SPIRIT MRS CRAY *sits in one corner and a* SPIRIT JACK *in another.* ATHENA *draws a large chalk circle then reads from her folder.*

ATHENA: 'A Learning Circle is a small self-managing, self-directed group that decides for itself its aims and objectives, and the outcomes it wants to achieve. There is no prescribed program to complete. It is *you*, the participants, who collectively decide the issues you want to focus on.'

MR MACK: [*offstage*] Hello! Anyone there?!

MR MACK *enters.*

ATHENA: Oh! Hello! Thanks for coming.

MR MACK *notices the empty hall.*

You're the first one here, besides me of course. I'm Athena.

MR MACK: Mr Mack.

ATHENA: Would you like a cup of tea?

MR MACK: No milk, no sugar.

ATHENA: Black.

MR MACK: Yes.

ATHENA: I haven't unpacked the tea and bickies yet, but I won't be too long.

MR MACK *gives an awkward nod as* ATHENA *scurries off.*

He enters the old bandstand. He walks up to the microphone, re-living a moment.

MR MACK: Welcome! Welcome! And…

OLD ELSA *enters.*

Humph! Didn't think *you'd* turn up.

OLD ELSA: Neither did I.

MR MACK: Always full of surprises.

OLD ELSA: Whadda ya mean by that?

MR MACK: Walking out and never coming back.

OLD ELSA: I'm here now.

MR MACK: Too bloody late!

OLD ELSA: I had my reasons.

MR MACK: Think I'll wait outside.

OLD ELSA: Mr Mack!

> MR MACK *exits.*

> OLD ELSA *takes to the bandstand and opens the piano. She plays a single note reprise of 'Soldier Boy' then closes the lid. She takes Jack's ribbon from her pocket.*

> *Musical intro: 'Soldier Boy'.*

> OLD ELSA *sings a duet with* SPIRIT JACK.

'SOLDIER BOY'

> [*Sung*] I could have been born in Paris and walk the Chaise de Lounge,
> I could have been sipping coffee and eating those little croissants,
> I could have been walking my poodle with French satin gloves,
> Instead I was born in Australia and it's here that I found love.

SOLDIERS: Hup! Two, three, four! Hup! Two, three, four!

OLD ELSA:

> I'm in love with a soldier boy,
> He's been redeployed
> To defend my heart from all of the boys,
> My wartime honey and me.

SOLDIERS: Hup! Two, three, four! Hup! Two, three, four!

SPIRIT JACK:

> She kisses my lips like a three-o-three,
> Parachute opens inside of me,
> Float to the ground happy to be,
> My sugar bunny and me.

OLD ELSA:

> When he walked down that gangplank
> My heart caught his eye,
> Her kisses were sweeter than
> Bully beef and apple pie.

> No more letters to a foreign land,
> We'll walk together hand in hand,
> One little baby sitting in a pram,
> My wartime honey and me.

SOLDIERS: Hup! Two, three, four! Hup! Two, three, four!

CHARLIE *enters. He stands in the doorway as* OLD ELSA *finishes the song.*

OLD ELSA:
> I'm in love with a soldier boy,
> He's been redeployed
> To defend my heart from all other boys,
> My wartime honey,
> My sugar bunny,
> My wartime honey and me.

SOLDIERS: Hup! Two, three, four! Hup! Two, three, four!

The song ends.

OLD ELSA: Charlie! I didn't see you there. You found a chemist, that's good.

OLD ELSA *takes the chemist bag and places it in her handbag.*

OLD CHARLIE: Just like old times, aye?

OLD ELSA: Not really.

CHARLIE *sulks.*

It's just a song.

CHARLIE *sulks.*

Oh, for goodness sake, I knew we shouldn't have come.

OLD CHARLIE: Whadda ya mean? It was your idea!

OLD ELSA: Don't start! I just copped a mouthful from Mr Mack.

OLD CHARLIE: And so did I!

ATHENA *and* MR MACK *enter.* ATHENA *is carrying a box with tea, milk, et cetera.*

ATHENA: It was well advertised. I even handed out flyers at the Survival Concert.

MR MACK: No-one cares anymore.

ATHENA: Should we wait for a few more people to…

MR MACK: Nah! Might as well go home.

ATHENA: I got money from the Reconciliation Council to organise this. I can't tell them nothing happened.

MR MACK: Waste of bloody time *and money*!

> OLD ELSA *waits for an introduction from* MR MACK *but he snubs them.*

OLD ELSA: I'm Elsa Runaway and this is my husband Charlie.

ATHENA: Glad to meet you, I'm Athena.

MR MACK: She's the one to blame for this!

ATHENA: Could you *please* stay an hour or so? I have to put *something* in the acquittal.

> OLD ELSA *looks at* OLD CHARLIE *who shrugs.*

Maybe some photos… of smiley faces?

> *They all look glum.*

Please? Mr Mack?

MR MACK: Alright!

ATHENA: Thank you. [*She opens her folder.*] Now before we start, we should have a welcome to country.

MR MACK: What?

ATHENA: Point number one, a welcome to country, you know the cultural thing you do. And seeing as the Reconciliation Council is sponsoring this, we should hold a Learning Circle.

OLD ELSA: Learning Circle?

ATHENA: I've marked it out with chalk. [*She reads from the folder.*] 'A Learning Circle is a small self-managing, self-directed group that decides for itself its aims and objectives and…'

MR MACK: Well, let's not be *selfish* and wait till a few *more* people turn up.

ATHENA: Oh!… Then could you put this banner up outside while we're waiting? It's part of the deal.

> MR MACK *pulls out a spring-loaded Reconciliation banner, which snaps back.*

MR MACK: Shit!

ATHENA: You'll need two people.

MR MACK: Mmmm.

OLD CHARLIE: How many months are ya?

OLD ELSA: Charlie! You don't ask those sorts of questions!

OLD CHARLIE: Why not?

MR MACK: She might be fat!

ATHENA: I'm four and half months.

MR MACK *picks up banner.*

MR MACK: Oy! Come on, you!

MR MACK *and* OLD CHARLIE *exit.*

OLD ELSA *feels awkward being left alone with* ATHENA.

OLD ELSA: First one?

ATHENA: And probably the last.

OLD ELSA: Really.

ATHENA: No partner, no father, just Gran.

OLD ELSA: And your mother?

ATHENA: Passed away when I was fifteen. Refused medical treatment and refused to slow down. Dragged me along to protest after protest, right till the end.

OLD ELSA: What sort of protests?

ATHENA: You name it! 'Land rights', 'Wood chipping', 'Save the whales'… 'Honk if you love Jesus'. The back of our Volvo was covered in stickers.

MR MACK *and* OLD CHARLIE *enter.*

MR MACK: It gets bulldozed tomorrow.

OLD CHARLIE *sucks his finger and shakes his hand.*

OLD CHARLIE: Bloody banner!

MR MACK: They'll put up a plaque recognising the fact that no blackfellas can be recognised around here anymore.

ATHENA: Foreshore redevelopment!

MR MACK: We should protest!

ATHENA: I can see the sticker now. 'Hands off the old hall!'

OLD CHARLIE: It's not worth saving this old dump!

MR MACK: Why did you bother coming? Ya never cared about this club!

OLD CHARLIE: Those days are finished.

MR MACK: That's because you stole my main—

OLD CHARLIE: I never stole nothing!

MR MACK: I shoulda booted you fair in the arse while I had the—
ATHENA: Excuse me! [*She waves her folder.*] Reconciliation!
MR MACK: Humph!

> OLD CHARLIE *and* MR MACK *glare at each other.*

ATHENA: I did some research about the club and found some old press clippings from a newspaper that—
OLD ELSA: Press clippings?

> MR MACK *grabs the photos.*

MR MACK: Give me a look.

> MR MACK *holds the clippings close to his chest like playing cards.*

OLD ELSA: Show them around!
MR MACK: Ah! Bingo! Here's a picture of you, Elsa, singing with… *Jack!*
ATHENA: Let me see!

> *She takes the clipping.*

[*To* OLD ELSA]You look so glamorous with your hair done up.
MR MACK: He was a good bloke Jack. Mmmm!

> OLD CHARLIE *glares at* MR MACK.

ATHENA: Was he someone special?
MR MACK: Salt of the earth!
ATHENA: You look like you were having fun.
MR MACK: Oh, they had fun alright!
ATHENA: What song were you singing?
OLD ELSA: I don't remember.
OLD CHARLIE: I remember a song! Me and Elsa's *special* song!

> *He grabs* OLD ELSA *and tries to dance with her whilst singing.*

[*Sung*] I've got eyes for someone but she's got eyes for no-one…
OLD ELSA: No, Charlie.
OLD CHARLIE: [*sung*] … except the man with the spurs, buckle, hat and curls…
OLD ELSA: Stop it!
OLD CHARLIE: [*sung*] … a cowgirl in love! I've got a coat…

> OLD ELSA *angrily pushes* OLD CHARLIE *away and snaps at him.*

OLD ELSA: Don't!

ATHENA: Mrs Runaway, are you okay?

OLD CHARLIE: You must remember *our* special song?

OLD ELSA: Come on, I've seen enough.

> OLD ELSA *hurries towards the exit, followed by* OLD CHARLIE.

MR MACK: Good riddance!

ATHENA: I need a photo before you go!

> OLD FAY *enters, carrying an urn.*

OLD FAY: Happy reunion, everybody!

ATHENA: Gran! You're late.

OLD ELSA: Gran?

OLD FAY: I thought I'd buy an urn for the occasion.

> ATHENA *places the urn by the bandstand.*

Elsa! So good to see you! Just like old times!

OLD ELSA: Goodbye.

OLD FAY: You're not leaving, are you? I've brought some wonderful old photos of Nanny to show you.

> OLD ELSA *stops in her tracks.*

Mr Mack! What a wonderful day it's going to be.

MR MACK: Ya reckon?

OLD CHARLIE: Let's get out of here.

OLD ELSA: No!

OLD CHARLIE: I thought you wanted to…

OLD ELSA: Not till I've seen the photos.

> OLD FAY *takes a scarf out of her handbag then puts it back in and takes out some biscuits.*

OLD FAY: Been such a long time, Charles. Here, I bought you some biscuits.

OLD ELSA: Fruit mince pillows, Charlie's favorite.

OLD FAY: What a wonderful idea to have a pre-demolition gathering.

OLD CHARLIE: Whose idea was it?

OLD FAY: Mine of course.

OLD ELSA: Where's the photos?

OLD FAY: In my bag.

OLD ELSA: Show me.

OLD FAY: All in good time.

OLD ELSA: Now!

OLD FAY: Excuse me! They're my family photos and I'll show them when I'm ready.

OLD ELSA: That's my mother!

OLD FAY: No disrespect, but she was my mother too.

OLD ELSA: She was your family's bloody slave.

OLD FAY: For goodness sake, get over it.

OLD ELSA: There's nothing to get over, she was my mother not yours.

OLD FAY: She wet-nursed me, and loved me like I was her daughter. Just accept it!

OLD ELSA: I'll never forgive your family for putting me in that bloody children's home!

OLD FAY: You can't blame my family! It was the right thing at the time!

OLD ELSA: Oh no! Couldn't let a baby get in the way of the cooking and cleaning and wiping your arse!

OLD FAY: If you want to blame someone, blame the Native Welfare!

OLD ELSA: I blame your family!

OLD FAY: At least you had the opportunity to become civilised!

ATHENA: Gran!

OLD CHARLIE: Civilised!

OLD ELSA: It's alright! Seeing as I'm now a… 'Civilised Native'… there's no need to argue.

OLD FAY: Good.

OLD ELSA: Because I'm the one with her blood in my veins! Not you!

OLD FAY: Blood means nothing! It was me that looked after her. Where were you, her so-called, 'daughter', when she was dying?!

MR MACK: What a rotten reunion this is!

ATHENA: I think it's fantastic! [*She reads from the folder.*] 'We should acknowledge the past no matter how confronting and traumatic it might be.' Let's strike while the iron's hot and form a Learning Circle. Come on now, gather round!

OLD FAY: A what?

MR MACK: Don't ask.

ATHENA: [*reading from the folder*] 'It's a small self-managing, self-directed group that decides for itself its aims and objectives, and the outcomes it wants to achieve. There is no prescribed program to complete. It is *you*, the participants, who collectively decide the issues you want to focus on.'

OLD CHARLIE: You two better make up before we get chucked in the circle.

OLD FAY: Alright! I'm sorry. I'm sorry, for calling you *civilised*.

OLD ELSA *considers her response.*

OLD ELSA: I… deeply regret our argument… but I'm not sorry for what I said.

MR MACK: Ya acting like spoilt little girls!

OLD FAY: I can see this is a waste of time. Goodbye!

MR MACK: [*to* OLD ELSA] The person you *should* be apologising to is ya mother, but it's too late for that!

MR MACK *and* OLD ELSA *continue their argument, as* ATHENA *and* OLD FAY *begin theirs.*

ATHENA: You pushed me into doing this so you can bloody well stay!

OLD ELSA: All I wanted was for her to live with me and Jack!

OLD FAY: Don't talk to me like that!

MR MACK: You broke her heart!

ATHENA: I'll talk to you however I want. I'm a woman now.

OLD ELSA: And she broke mine!

OLD FAY: I want to live at uni, Gran. Oops! I'm pregnant, Gran. Can I come home, Gran?!

MR MACK: She never performed after that!

ATHENA: I'll leave if you want!

OLD ELSA: That's all you we're worried about! Your bloody club!

OLD FAY: At least I'd get some peace and quiet!

MR MACK: And you, Charlie Runaway! You stole my main act!

OLD CHARLIE *raises a chair above his head and aims it towards* MR MACK *who shields himself.*

OLD CHARLIE: Arrrgh!

OLD ELSA: No, Charlie!

ATHENA *screams.* FAY *gasps.*

OLD CHARLIE *slams the chair down in the Learning Circle.*

OLD CHARLIE: No-one's leaving!

He grabs another chair and slams it in the Circle.

Athena, do your worst!

Everyone begrudgingly takes a chair and sits in the Circle.

ATHENA: Huh, hmmm! Now, as the facilitator, I think we should skip the… warm welcomes and cut to the chase. I'd like everyone to be totally honest and say what you really feel, in your heart of hearts, about black and white relations in Australia. Now who's going to go first?

No-one offers.

Mr Mack?

MR MACK: Nu-huh!

ATHENA: Gran?

OLD FAY: Whatever I say is going to sound old-fashioned and *they'll* probably shoot me down in flames anyway.

ATHENA: As the facilitator, I'd ask everyone to respect Gran's opinions!

OLD ELSA: Hmmm.

OLD CHARLIE: Alright.

MR MACK: Humph!

ATHENA: Good. Go on, Gran.

OLD FAY: I think there are some wonderful ambassadors for the Aborigine race. Your sportsmen and your personalities are wonderful role models for young people and recently when I was at Ayers Rock I saw some *real* Aborigines painting and—

ATHENA: Gran! You can't say that.

OLD FAY: But I thought I could say whatever I wanted in the Circle.

ATHENA: It's the Noble Savage Syndrome.

OLD CHARLIE: All muscley and athletic from hunting, and look, when they're on TV they can make us laugh! Just don't talk to them in the street!

MR MACK: Hang on a minute! Our footy players are doing a bloody good job!

ATHENA: Maybe you've been *indoctrinated* into the white man's way of thinking, like Gran!

MR MACK: I haven't been doctored and I thought you said we had to respect her opinions.

ATHENA: As the facilitator I can make judgments in the interests of the—

OLD CHARLIE: How bloody patronising is that! Don't let the natives get restless!

ATHENA: If you think it's a racist issue, it might be because of your— Hang on a minute!

She consults her folder as everyone waits for her response.

Poor Bugger Me Syndrome!

OLD ELSA: Oh, oh!

OLD CHARLIE: How dare you accuse me of that! You're the one with all the bloody syndromes!

MR MACK: Settle down! Settle down! Athena, I think you'd better try a different way of running this ring.

ATHENA: I'm sorry, Mr Runaway, I never meant for any of my comments to be taken personally.

OLD CHARLIE: Hmmm.

ATHENA: From now on, don't think of me as a 'white person' or the 'facilitator', or even 'Athena'.

OLD FAY: What then?

ATHENA: Think of me as the… 'devil's advocate'.

OLD ELSA: God help us with you on his side.

ATHENA: So you believe in God, do you?

OLD ELSA *is suspicious of* ATHENA*'s question.*

OLD ELSA: Sometimes prayer gives me comfort.

ATHENA: How comfortable was it when they rammed religion down your throat in the Children's Home?

OLD CHARLIE: Now that's enough!

ATHENA: And beat you for speaking your language!

OLD CHARLIE: Pull back, girl!

OLD ELSA: All you know is from bumper stickers, young lady!

ATHENA: That doesn't mean I have to bury my head in the sand and pretend these issues don't exist!

OLD ELSA: I know they exist because I lived it! I'm a member of the Stolen Generation. While you're grandmother was being spoonfed I was scrubbing floors and freezing all night in those bloody dormitories. If you were Stolen Generation you might—

OLD CHARLIE: Hang on a minute! I was taken away too but I don't run around acting like I'm a member of some exclusive club.

OLD ELSA: Charlie!

OLD CHARLIE: I'm sorry, but it's not who we are and I'm not gonna wear another government label around my neck. We're *people* first, and the rest is *just* something very bad that happened to us.

OLD ELSA: There's nothing *just* about it!

OLD FAY: Bad things can happen to anyone. I lost my daughter to breast cancer and—

OLD ELSA: At least you didn't have her stolen from you like my mother did!

OLD FAY: I did, by cancer!

MR MACK: This Circle is bullshit!

MR MACK *storms out of the Circle.*

ATHENA: Mr Mack?… Mr Mack, come back into the Circle.

MR MACK: No!

ATHENA: It's alright for us to get angry.

MR MACK: I don't need to be in a Circle to get angry!

OLD CHARLIE: Maybe that's the problem. No-one gets angry anymore.

OLD FAY: The fire's turned to ash. And the ash has blown away.

ATHENA: Please, Mr Mack? I'll give you a bumper sticker.

MR MACK: Alright.

MR MACK *re-enters the Circle.*

ATHENA *consults her folder.*

ATHENA: I'd like to try some visualisation. Now close your eyes and imagine Aboriginal people are eighty percent of the population. You have your treaty… and your land back!

OLD FAY: So now I have to give them my house?

ATHENA: Oh, Gran! You just ruined it!

OLD FAY: Look what's going on in Africa.

ATHENA: At least in Africa they called it *Truth* and Reconciliation but here they just called it Reconciliation because it's got nothing to do with the truth!

MR MACK: I'll tell ya something for nothing! In the club days it was whitefellas and blackfellas all with a common purpose, *hope* for a better future and *faith* that it would happen. Now all I see is an empty old hall.

OLD CHARLIE: It's not about the hall. It's what people took away from here that's important: dignity, pride and community. It didn't matter where you came from, we was all one family. Just like the old cultural ways through skin names. Everyone fitted into either Banaka, Burungu, Milangka or Garimarra. My mother was a Banaka so I'm a Burungu. That's what made us one family. Just like the club.

They ponder.

Funny that. It's the first time I've spoken my language since they took me.

ATHENA: That's not funny, Mr Runaway. That's very sad.

MR MACK: We need to clean up our own backyard before we start knocking down the neighbours' fence.

ATHENA: My generation is much more educated and enlightened! We won't make the same mistakes in formulating policies for indigenous people! We know what needs to be done for *you*!

MR MACK: Is that so!

Musical intro: 'Shin Stew'.

OLD TOSS *enters. He sits on a chair in the Circle with* ATHENA *on his knee. He thrusts his hand up her back and she becomes a ventriloquist doll.*

OLD TOSS: *Welcome to my circle!* Now there's been a lot of conniving going on in Australia, and that word 'conniving' comes from the word 'k-nife', and to cut a John Dory short we've been k-nifed in the back.

ATHENA: Hee hee hee! You said... k-nifed!

OLD TOSS: Kn-oath! History has dealt its hand with a card up every sleeve and shuffled the legislation so the world couldn't see. Now the true history of Australia is about to be revealed. By me! Old Toss! With the future on my Aborigi-k-nee!

OLD TOSS *sings.*

'SHIN STEW'

OLD TOSS: [*sung*]
    You're a happy little vegemite with paint upon your cheeks,
    Wandering round the bush for over forty thousand years,
    But that just ain't good enough; we know what's good for you,

ALL:
    We're gonna have to cook you up in our little stew.

ATHENA: What sort of a stew is it?

OLD TOSS: It's a shin stew.

ATHENA: What do you put in a shin stew?

They sing 'shin' words.

OLD TOSS: [*sung*]

Well you...

Start with colonisa-*tion* to soften up the meat,

Then miscegena-*tion* to whiten up the cheeks,

Then assimila-*tion* to make you fit right in,

ALL:

Then reconcilia-*tion* to forgive us of our sins.

ATHENA *sniffs the stew.*

ATHENA: It smells awful!

OLD TOSS: That's because it's a crock of shit...

[*Sung*] Now we've taken out the culture and the language too,

Now that you've been cooking in our little stew,

The government now owns your land your sites have been destroyed,

ALL:

It's off to jail forever, you naughty little boy!

ATHENA: I think I've had enough of this shin stew!

OLD TOSS: We're not finished yet!

OLD TOSS's *arm is looking for something inside* ATHENA's *guts.*

ATHENA: What ya doing, Old Toss?

OLD TOSS: Hang on a minute... here we go!

OLD TOSS *pulls out* ATHENA's *heart.*

ATHENA: You've ripped my heart out!

OLD TOSS: Extremely right!

[*Sung*] Well, now we've ripped your heart out you'll never ever bleed,

It's hard to show affection or raise a family,

For statistical purposes we'll keep you on our files,

ALL:

And when we've bred the colour out we'll chuck you on the pile.

The song ends.

ATHENA: I don't want to taste this stew! It looks terrible!

OLD TOSS: It's guaranteed to leave a bitter taste in ya mouth!

ATHENA: Can't we just have dessert?!

OLD TOSS: That's the problem, my girl, everyone wants to trifle without tasting the stew!

Musical outro: 'Shin Stew'.

OLD TOSS *exits.*

OLD FAY: I've had enough of this. We're just going round and round in circles in the Circle and all this political correctness is giving me hives!

MR MACK: Let's get back to what we came here for.

OLD ELSA: And what's that?

MR MACK: A happy pre-demolition.

ATHENA *flicks through her folder.*

ATHENA: I don't think we've covered all the points.

MR MACK: *Ngalluk jurapiny wanju nunnuk ngallah Noongar Boodja. Nitjah ngallah moorts Boodja koorah koorah.*

OLD FAY: What was that?

MR MACK: It's a welcome to Noongar country.

ATHENA: Thank you, Mr Mack. *We're* deeply honoured.

OLD FAY: Here you are, Elsa. You're *welcome* to look at these.

OLD FAY *hands a thankless* OLD ELSA *the photographs.* OLD ELSA *looks through them.*

ATHENA: Look at these bathing suits. Oh my God, she's got a Union Jack on her bum!

MR MACK: I remember that night.

ATHENA: Is that you, Mr Runaway?

OLD CHARLIE: Yep, that's me alright. I was the judge.

ATHENA: Very photogenic!

MR MACK: It's just out of focus.

OLD CHARLIE: Some people thought I looked like Humphrey Bogart in that hat.

MR MACK: Maybe when he was pulling that boat through the mud.

OLD FAY: Do you remember this, Mr Mack?

OLD FAY *slowly takes a scarf out of her bag.*

MR MACK: I remember that scarf. It's from that striptease ya did that night.

ATHENA: Striptease! Go, Gran!

MR MACK: Oh! I'm sorry, Elsa, that was the night Jack passed away.

OLD ELSA: It could have been worse… I could have seen Fay's striptease.

MR MACK: What a night that was!

OLD CHARLIE *slips off his chair and holds his heart.*

OLD FAY: Goodness! Are you alright, Charles?

OLD ELSA: Charlie!

MR MACK *and* ELSA *assist* CHARLIE *back onto his seat.*

OLD CHARLIE: Bit too much excitement. I'll be right in a while.

ATHENA: Should I call an ambulance?

OLD CHARLIE: Stop fussing, I'm fine!

OLD ELSA: His ticker's not too good. Had rheumatic fever when he was a kid.

MR MACK: Sit there and take deep breaths.

OLD ELSA: I'll get ya pills and some water. Now where's my bag?

OLD FAY: I'll sit with you for a while.

ATHENA: We'll set up for the photos. Grab some chairs, Mr Mack!

MR MACK *moves some chairs as* ATHENA *puts up a flag and* OLD ELSA *goes to get pills and water.*

OLD CHARLIE: So, what was that all about?

OLD FAY: What?

OLD CHARLIE: The bloody scarf!

OLD FAY: It's just a little memento.

OLD CHARLIE: What are you up to?

OLD FAY: Why didn't you ever contact me?

OLD CHARLIE: I didn't know you wanted to see me.

OLD FAY: I could have put you in jail, Charles, or even worse, had you hanged.

OLD CHARLIE: And I appreciate you keeping quiet.

OLD FAY: You could have at least found the time to explain to me what happened that night!

OLD CHARLIE: I tried to at the club but you didn't wanna listen!

OLD FAY: There was plenty of time afterwards.

OLD CHARLIE: We had to get on with our lives.

OLD FAY: Have you told anyone?

OLD CHARLIE: There's nothing to tell and why are you bringing this up now?

OLD FAY: Because I cherish what this club stood for and what *you said* we took away from here, dignity and pride. If you killed Jack, I need to know you had no choice; otherwise, I'm as guilty as you are.

OLD CHARLIE: There's *nothing* for either of us to feel guilty about.

OLD FAY: Does Elsa know?

OLD CHARLIE: It would only upset her.

OLD FAY: Tell her, Charles, if not for your sake, for mine, Jack and Elsa's.

> OLD FAY *throws the scarf on* OLD CHARLIE*'s lap. He holds it with repulsion.*

ATHENA: Mr Runaway! Is this flag straight?… Mr Runaway?

MR MACK: The red should be on the bottom. How can we have reconciliation when they keep hanging our flag upside down?

> OLD ELSA *approaches with the pills and water. She notices* OLD CHARLIE *is holding the scarf.*

OLD ELSA: Well, this looks very cozy.

OLD FAY: I'm sorry?

OLD ELSA: Stop flirting with my man!

OLD FAY: What *are* you talking about?

OLD ELSA: I'm talking about biscuits, cozy conversations and scarves! That's what!

> OLD ELSA *places the pills and water next to* OLD CHARLIE *then throws the biscuits.* OLD FAY *stands.* OLD ELSA *knocks over a chair.* MR MACK *jumps in between.*

MR MACK: Hey! Hey! Hey! You're not in the Learning Circle now!

OLD FAY: I'm not the least bit interested in Charles! If you want to know what we we're talking about I'm sure Charles—

OLD ELSA: Don't try and shift the blame! You've been chasing him all your life. You stole my mother and now you're still trying to steal my man!

OLD FAY: Oh, so we're back to that again, are we! For your information, dear, I was over Charles the night you said yes, and believe it or not I had a loving marriage and a devoted husband. God rest his soul!

MR MACK: As far as I'm concerned, you're both sisters! That's how ya mum treated ya! You might not be blood sisters but you're still *bloody* sisters and ya need to start treating each other with a little more respect! I'm gonna… plug in the urn!

MR MACK *exits.*

OLD CHARLIE *remains seated but worried.*

OLD FAY: Sisters?

OLD ELSA: Impossible!

ATHENA: Why not?

OLD ELSA: Don't listen to him, he's just an old fool.

ATHENA: Didn't you ever wish you had a sister?

OLD FAY *looks to* OLD ELSA.

OLD FAY: There were times when I…

OLD ELSA: Never!

OLD FAY: … when I wish I'd had a sister!

OLD ELSA: We have nothing in common!

ATHENA: You both shared the same mother's love.

OLD ELSA: It was her duty.

OLD FAY: It was more than that. She loved both of—

OLD ELSA: She loved no-one.

OLD FAY: I don't believe that for one minute.

ATHENA: How could anyone doubt a mother's love?

Silence.

I wish I had my mother back. If only to see my baby born.

OLD FAY: You've got me. I've been your gran and your mother.

ATHENA: If you were sisters I'd have two grans and two mothers!

OLD FAY: I'm your blood grandmother and that's enough!

ATHENA: Family is more than blood. You said that yourself!

OLD FAY: You just want one of those Aborigine skin names.

ATHENA: I'm having my first baby, and to be honest, I'm scared stiff. If you weren't around Gran I'd have no-one. Can't you make up, for my sake?

OLD FAY *looks expectantly to* OLD ELSA.

OLD FAY: I guess none of us are getting any younger.

ATHENA *slowly approaches* OLD ELSA.

ATHENA: Would you like to have a feel, Nanna Elsa, the baby's kicking?

OLD ELSA *reaches out but stops and becomes stoic.*

OLD FAY: Come on, Athena, you don't have to humiliate yourself.

MR MACK *enters.*

OLD ELSA *directs her tirade at* ATHENA *and rips up her folder.*

OLD ELSA: It's was my mother that was humiliated. It's do-gooders like you that make me sick! And you're just as bad as the worst of them with your stupid folder and Learning Circle. You're nothing but a spoilt little bitch who knows nothing about anything! You can look after your bloody child yourself because I'm not gonna be your baby's black nanny!

ATHENA *'s lip quivers. She back off and sits crying.*

A moment of silence as OLD ELSA *realises she went too far.*

OLD FAY: This is no longer an issue between us. You had no right to take your rubbish out on her. Shame on you! I hope I never see you again!

OLD FAY *goes to comfort* ATHENA.

OLD CHARLIE *looks away and* MR MACK *shakes his head in disgust.*

OLD ELSA *approaches* ATHENA.

Underscore: 'Rainbow Colours'.

OLD ELSA: Athena, I'm sorry. I never had a mother to show me any affection or even do the little things like brush my hair. Even when I found her, I couldn't be with her. I don't know what happened in her life but she couldn't even put her arms around me. Every night I'd dream of the day we'd be together and everything would be right again, but it never came.

OLD ELSA *sings.*

'RAINBOW COLOURS'

> [*Sung*] There's a dream on my pillow tonight,
> Waiting for me to turn off the light.
> Rainbow colours in my mind,
> Paint a picture of a better life.
> Someone to warm me in a winter storm,
> Someone to comfort when I'm all alone.
> Autumn leaves brown and grey,
> Rainbow colours just wash them away.

Instrumental.

SPIRIT MRS CRAY *walks up to* ELSA *and gives her a hug.*

ATHENA & ELSA: [*together*]
> There's a dream on my pillow tonight,
> Waiting for me to turn off the light.
> Rainbow colours in my mind,
> Paint a picture of a better life.

The song ends.

OLD FAY *and* OLD ELSA *stand either side of* ATHENA. OLD ELSA *feels the baby kick.*

MR MACK: He might be one of those footballers we was talking about.

OLD ELSA: Or a pretty little girl, with a red ribbon in her hair!

MR MACK: I'm sorry if I was a bit hard ya, Elsa. Anyways, I'd like youse all to take a memento from this hall with you.

MR MACK *holds out his hand.* ATHENA *has a look.*

ATHENA: Rusty old nails?

MR MACK: I pulled them out of the floorboards in the kitchen.

OLD FAY: What am I going to do with a rusty old nail?

MR MACK: Get ya belly button pierced! [*He goes to the bandstand.*] Now we didn't get much of a turnout but I think the ones that were meant to be here, are here.

ATHENA: Here, here!

MR MACK *holds up a nail.*

MR MACK: It might *be* just a rusty old nail, but it's been forged in steel. Just like the bonds we still have after all these years. It might *be* just a rusty old nail but it held this hall together, just like the people who worked hard to hold the club together. And finally, even nails can break and rust away, so I'd like to dedicate this reunion not only to the ones that are present, but also to those who couldn't be here with us: Mrs Cray and Jack.

One by one they take a nail, except OLD CHARLIE.

ATHENA: Mr Runaway?

OLD CHARLIE *picks up the pills, looks at them then puts them down. He walks onto the bandstand to make a speech.*

Underscore: 'Love the Love You Love'.

OLD CHARLIE: I'd just like to say that Jack was my brother and Elsa's husband. After I left the mission I was living in the camps along the railway. His father took me in and treated me like I was his son. Me and Jack was very close. When he got back from the war his mind was gone. He wasn't the same. Tried to kill his pain with the drink and medicines.

> OLD CHARLIE *picks up a nail and clenches it. He sings.*

'LOVE THE LOVE YOU LOVE'

> [*Sung*] May you never feel like I do,
> The deepest darkest blue,
> With the cold wind of fate across my back,
> May you never feel like I feel,
> The coldest hardest steel
> Running like a blade across my heart.
> May your love never grow old,
> May your words never grow cold,
> May you sing the song and love the love you love.
> May the words in your heart
> Part the seas, light the dark,
> As you dream the dream and love the love you love.

> *Instrumental underscores* OLD CHARLIE.

You see, a fight broke out between us, right here, right inside this circle. We got arrested and had another fight back in the lockup. He told me he couldn't go on the way it was. He knew that one night, when he was having one of his nightmares, he'd kill Elsa. I couldn't let my brother kill the woman... we both loved.

> SPIRIT JACK *comes over and places his arm around a broken* CHARLIE. *He sings.*

SPIRIT JACK: [*sung*]

> Let your life be full of lovin',
> Let your loving be full of life,
> Let the bad times make the good times shine like gold.
> May you wash away with tears
> The memories that you fear,
> And your dreams let you taste what might have been.

> May your love never grow old,
> May your words never grow cold,
> May you sing the song and love the love you love.
> May the words in your heart
> Part the seas, light the dark,
> As you dream the dream and love the love you love.

OLD CHARLIE:

> May you never feel like I do,
> The deepest darkest blue,
> With the cold wind of fate across my back.

The song ends.

SPIRIT JACK *takes* OLD CHARLIE *to the Marble Bar pool.*

Transition.

Underscore: 'Waltzing the Wilarra'.

Lighting effects of water stars and the Wilarra moon overhead.

I'm standing with my mother beneath the paperbarks, at the edge of the Marble Bar pool. The night is so still the stars float on the water. I look across the pool, and the stars and the Wilarra shine so brightly, I can't tell where the night sky ends and the pool begins. I'm standing in the universe… in the womb… of my mother.

The cast sing.

'WALTZING THE WILARRA'

ALL: [*sung*]

> Waltzing the Wilarra tonight,
> Million stars of candlelight,
> Shadows dancing silver blue,
> Golden sunrise comes too soon,
> And all the lovers who've travelled so far
> Give their hearts to the Wilarra.

Repeat.

The song ends and the lights fade.

As the cast assembles for a curtain call, they sing encores of 'I've Got Eyes' and 'Wheatbelt Boogie'.

Finally, MR MACK *steps forward.*

MR MACK: And the winner of the bathing suit competition is… Old Toss!

OLD TOSS *parades his swimsuit.*

THE END

www.ingramcontent.com/pod-product-compliance
Lightning Source LLC
Chambersburg PA
CBHW041934090426
42744CB00017B/2055